# Queen Bee

The Art of Attracting Men

Manhardeep Singh

Copyright © Manhardeep Singh

All rights reserved.

ISBN: 979-8-68-871010-6

# CONTENTS

| | | |
|---|---|---|
| 1 | Becoming Queen Bee | 1 |
| 2 | The Essence of Being a Woman | 5 |
| 3 | Battle of the Sexes | 7 |
| 4 | The Mighty Power of Influence | 11 |
| 5 | What Men Really Want? | 15 |
| 6 | Women Speak but Men Don't Listen | 19 |
| 7 | Empowering Your Man | 23 |
| 8 | Men will be Men | 27 |
| 9 | Conquering the Bed | 29 |
| 10 | Final Words | 33 |

## ೫ 1 ೪

## Becoming Queen Bee

The term queen bee usually refers to an adult, female that lives in a honey beehive. There is normally only one queen bee in a hive, in which case the bees will usually follow and fiercely protect her. If you ask yourself what type of girl do men adore and couldn't live without today, what the answer would be? I bet it would include reference to a celebrity actress or a blond, blue-eyes female with killer legs. Well, this type of woman would get a lot of attention, but she isn't the type of woman that men adore.

Now, that's really good news for most!

You see, men are visual creatures and that first attraction is sparked from looks. I bet, you would be taken aback to find out what men actually want from women.

In a recent study conducted by a team of sociologists, they were able to determine a common denominator that men found attractive in women. The one thing that would get any guy to fall for her. You would never guess what that one denominator is. If you think it is her breasts, her legs or her bum, then you are wrong. In fact, it isn't even any body part. Neither, it is her features.

The one thing that attracts every guy is her smile. Yes. Majority of men confirmed that they found thing as attractive as a woman's smile.

The point is to put the preconceived notions to a side. Put the rules society has beaten into you to a side. It needs to be stressed that men and women are different and it's okay to be a woman. It is okay to give up control to your partner once in a while. Losing control to your partner will make you feel better as well.

Society may have given equal footing for men and women in the workplace and other areas of lives. It is true that a woman can do almost anything a can, and vice-versa. It is also true that there are some fundamental differences that have been hardwired. The problem arises when we overlook those differences. The problem arises when we consider that those differences do not exist. Women end up shutting themselves away from the world to be more like the men they feel they need to compete with.

Generally, you will see such behaviour prevalent in the workplace. But, unfortunately, a lot of women carry the same behaviour over into the personal lives. With this behaviour, they end up hurting themselves as well as their partners.

Today, women are often afraid to be women. They are afraid to appear feminine or vulnerable. This is because they equate being vulnerable with being weak. But, quite the opposite is true. A woman who is in tune with herself and shows her vulnerability has more power over a man than the one who constantly acts tough.

This book will help explore the various differences between men and women. It will also highlight how those differences give more strength than any rules the society may seek to impose. Lastly, once you allow your inner woman to shine, then you become the girl that all men adore.

QUEEN BEE

## ꞌ 2 ꞋꞋ

## The Essence of Being a Woman

A lot of problems in relationships come from lack of understanding. In simpler words, there is no idea why guys act the way they do. In fact, often even they don't know why they act the way they do. So it's no surprise to find it difficult to decipher their responses.

This is one of the fundamental differences between men and women. But, before we begin to explore these differences further, it is worth taking to take a step back and look at yourself. Take a look at yourself in the mirror. It is vital to learn to accept who and what you are. Until then you can never make the necessary change to become the woman men adore. The biggest challenge is in how you see yourself, the perception about yourself.

The whole women's liberation has been taken to a whole new level from that women should have equal rights to men in society, to women should not be women and should act more like men. There is a simple reason behind this shift. Men are naturally competitive, women are not. So, to grow in the workplace, more and more women have to become as competitive as men, and in many cases, even more. Unfortunately, though, many women have taken this competition to a new level. Their drive to succeed has convinced them that being women means being weak. So, they shut off their feelings and act more like men.

Sadly, women are mistaken in their perception of considering femininity a weakness. In actuality, it is strength. It is the one thing that allows women to influence men much more effectively. Argument will not, competition will not. Men get disarmed by a woman's softness. This is because men were designed to fight and women, to nurture. This is the essence of being a woman.

## ಶೋ 3 ಡಃ

## Battle of the Sexes

What many women don't understand is that men are completely different. They process information differently. They relate to one another differently. They express differently. In such a case, a woman who understands these differences becomes a priceless gem that men adore. It is these exact functional differences between men and women that spark passion and love. Otherwise, why would they need each other?

### Understanding Men

Yes, despite the mystery of why men do what they do, it is possible to understand them. And it is probably easier for women to understand them than the other way around. To understand them, the first thing to know is that men are primarily driven by success and accomplishment. They weigh and value tangible results, efficiency and power. Everything they do is geared towards proving themselves.

Men are not the creatures who would sit and talk about their feelings. They are competitive and prefer to engage in competitive activities where they can win. It satisfies their innate need to feel superior over other males, to be the alpha male. In the same context, you won't find men reading People or Cosmo. Instead, their reading would include sports section of the paper or the news. They care little about romance novels because they are more into things than feelings. They like things that help them express power. It can be in the form of fancy sports car or the latest gadgets and gizmos.

**Solutions vs Advice**

Men are goal-driven. They feel good when they achieve goals. Because achieving goals proves that they are worthy and competent. If they accomplish on their own then that is an even greater testament to their power and strength.

Men are hardwired to solve their problems on their own. So, you will rarely find them talking about their problems. But when they do, it means they genuinely need advice and help.

If you can understand this side of men, then you'll understand why men hate being corrected or advised without asking for it. Such uncalled for advises makes them feel incompetent. They feel that you don't believe in their ability to solve the problem. This is also the reason why men offer solutions when you share your problems with them. This natural inclination to provide solution comes from the fact that if another man were to share his problems, it is an unspoken request for help, so he feels honoured to provide a solution.

When a man provides solution for the woman he loves, it is his expression of love. But when a woman gets upset perceiving that he isn't listening or empathizing, he has no idea what he did to upset her. The end result is that he withdraws and blocks her out.

## Dealing with Stress

Men and women both deal with stress differently. A woman will talk about her problems with her friends. Her friends will instinctively know that she needs little support and understanding, so they empathize. But, men tend to withdraw and focus on a different activity. This is done to tune out their problems until the day when they have to handle them.

But, most women think that he doesn't care about her, or is ignoring her because he isn't sharing his problems with her. Where in actuality, it is simply a matter of understanding how men deal with stress. It is also an important point to consider that it is as unrealistic to expect a man to open up immediately to you when he is stressed as it is for a man to expect you to calm down and be rational all the time.

The point to understand is that the next time he withdraws to watch football or read the newspaper; it doesn't mean he doesn't love you. It simply means he is very stressed. Learn to not take it personally and give him space. Let him fight his battles. Also, if you ask for his attention in a calm, relaxed manner, he will be more responsive than if you start the blame game.

## ॐ 4 ॐ

## The Mighty Power of Influence

Women seem to think that best way to influence their partners is either by nagging, yelling or shutting down when it seems that he is ignoring. The problem, though, lies that women expect men to read their minds and understand what they want from them. But, it is a path that will certainly lead to the relationship turmoil. It would be for the simple reasons that men are different in how they process feelings and emotions.

Take for instance, a woman want to talk about her problems, whereas men tend to withdraw and like to figure out solutions to their problems on their own. For a man to talk to someone about his problems usually means he is asking for advice or a solution. That is why when women share their problems, men tend to offer solutions. The thing is when women are sharing their problems, they don't want to hear a solution. They just want to be heard, understood and held. Women want someone to empathize. This is where lies the difference.

Men do not know how to empathize. It isn't how they are designed. When guys talk to each other about their problems, it is a sign that they are asking for advice or a solution. They certainly aren't asking for an understanding "Hmmm" and a hug, like women expect. So, when he offers a solution, his woman gets upset that he doesn't understand what she wants without actually realizing that he simply doesn't know.

But, there is a "weapon" that women possess, to influence men. It is their vulnerability. By opening your heart up and expressing the feelings you feel, you will be surprised at the results you will get. Do not mistake vulnerability as a weakness. Because allowing yourself to be vulnerable means that you are strong enough to risk getting hurt by opening up. When you allow yourself be vulnerable and express your emotions, you will look after yourself more because you will share with him exactly what you want and need.

There are very few things that make a man

happier than knowing that he can make his woman feel good. When you are upset, he wants to do everything in his ability and power to make you feel better. If you can genuinely express your feelings to him rather than rattle off a list of problems then you will that he will become more receptive.

# QUEEN BEE

## ॐ 5 ॐ

## What Men Really Want?

The first thing you need to understand about men is that they like things to be simple. They do not overanalyze every phrase you say looking for a hidden meaning nor they speak in riddles for you to solve. In fact, in most cases, you can be certain that when a man says something, that's exactly what he means in that moment.

How this can be used? It can be used to understand that men adore women who tell them straight what they feel and don't feel. For instance, instead of hinting that you are too tired to go out that evening, or trying to hint that you are upset because he isn't spending enough time with you, try telling him. Yes, this entails the risk of being rejected but you are also showing him what you want. There is nothing men love more than not having to worry about making a mistake and upsetting you.

Needless to say, the delivery of message is as important as the message itself. A man will respond much better if you deliver your message in a soft and feminine manner than shouting at him. You disarm him when you become soft and feminine. This is because of the innate desire of men to make their women happy. On the opposite side, if you start off by yelling, all you are doing is competing with him. He will start treating you like one of the guys, because guys compete against each other. So delivering the message by yelling at him will either make him do his "guy thing" and withdraw, or he will try to compete with you. Both these results are not in your favour.

Understand, men marry women who make them feel good. This is because they have trouble accessing their own emotions. Men love being with a woman who makes them feel good. If he is constantly walking around on eggshells because he doesn't know how to please you, the last thing he will feel is good.

**Men Want to Feel Needed**

Because of the structure of the society, many women are embarrassed to admit that they want to feel cherished and that they need a man. It's almost a sacrilege to admit it, even though they feel empty within without a partner.

You will find many women who have a great career and date all the time but have a hard time maintaining a relationship. They have no idea why are they caught in this vicious circle. It is because of the fact that they have convinced themselves that they don't need a man and that is what they naturally project.

If a man doesn't feel that a woman needs him, he will think that there is nothing he can do for her that she can't do on her own. He won't be able to play his role of the knight in the shiny armour for his woman. There is nothing that will get a man to run away faster than feeling that he isn't needed.

Talking about independence, it is a great thing in some areas of life, but it is the biggest killer of intimacy. Think about it: would you want to be with someone who doesn't need you?

You need to understand that the idea of equality is highly over rated in relationships. Consider, if you are both on equal footing then you would be like one of his mates. The fact is very few women want to be treated like one of the guys. Guys never open up to each other. They are constantly competing on some level or the other. They certainly don't hug or kiss each other. Is that what you want in your relationship?

## ಖ 6 ಅ

## Women Speak but Men Don't Listen

When women are upset with their man, they think the best solution is to get him to sit down and talk about it. She'll start talking a mile-a-minute and her man will eventually tune her out. Then she will get upset that he isn't listening to her. Then he gets more confused about why she is complaining because "I can tell you everything you said."

You need to engrave the following phrase in your mind: MEN HAVE SHORT ATTENTION SPANS. You see, men have this habit of presuming that every issue you talk about is in some way his fault. He will then try to explain himself, which will make you angrier and then the discussion turns into a shouting match.

Men don't respond to shouting because it is a form of competition. But, men do respond seeing their woman in pain. They do so tenfold if they feel that she isn't blaming them for her pain. Men will move mountains to put a smile back on the face of the woman they love.

So what's the takeaway? Instead of launching into a long explanation about what is upsetting you, which will have him eventually tune out soon after you start, try a different approach. Tell him what you feel in simple words. Keep it short and sweet. You will find that he responds much better and will be much more motivated to correct whatever he might be doing that is upsetting you.

Another way to get his attention is to simply walk away and keep your distance. Yes, initially he will be fine but soon he will start wondering if you are upset with him, then he will come to you. When that happens, he will be more receptive than if you had to force him to sit down and have "the talk."

## Men Don't Want to Compete With Their Woman

Men really don't want to compete with their woman. They don't marry for competition because they get enough of that in other areas of their lives, from work to their friends. What they want is someone they can confide in, someone they can have fun with and someone who will be loyal to them.

Men want peace. They want to please their wife or girlfriend. This is the reason why men avoid conflict in their relationships as best they can. Conflict, for a man, equates to a competition and men are hardwired to do everything they can to win any competition. Since most men don't want to win over their mate, they will end up withdrawing.

So, if you take a different approach, such as refusing to argue and, instead, use your feelings to disarm him, you will find that you are actually the one in control. Think about it, when you were a little girl and you wanted to get something from your Dad, what did you do? You used your feelings, making him feel like the best father on the planet and you would twirl him around your little finger, no matter how much trouble he would get into. It was all to make his little girl happy and put a smile on her face because it made him feel good.

The same holds true in relationships and if you can relearn the art of using your feelings, you will find that your man is much more responsive to you. He will want to do things for you simply to please you and see you happy because that is what makes him happy. There's nothing more important to a man than the knowledge that he can please his woman.

## ৪০ 7 ෬

## Empowering Your Man

Women love to try and change men. Go on, admit it, you know you do. How many times have you watched a movie and fallen for the bad guy and deep down "knew" you could change him? Just think of American Psycho starring Christian Bale. Millions of women were drooling over a psychotic killer brandishing a chainsaw and not simply because he looked good, but because deep down inside they were convinced they could change him.

Trying to change your man will only serve to push him away. Men feel empowered and loved when they are trusted and accepted for who they are. In fact, a little appreciation goes a long way to make him feel loved.

However, if you try to change him, in his mind you are basically saying that he isn't good enough, competent enough, smart enough and so on and so forth. The result is that you will be hurting him even if you don't realize it. The more you try to change him, the less he feels loved. The lesser he feels that you trust and accept him the way he is.

Here is where the fundamental difference plays its role. Women consider it a sign of affection to offer advice. Men see it as a validation of the fact that they aren't trusted. Remember, men are receptive to advice only when they ask for it.

So instead of trying to change him, show your love by offering him trust. You need to trust him for his capability of resolving his problems by himself.

This doesn't mean you should hide your feelings. It simply means that you shouldn't use them as punishment or a weapon to change him. You won't succeed in changing him rather it will drive the two of you apart.

For example, if he is upset, you might be tempted to prod and poke until you get the truth out of him about what's bothering him. However, he will see that as an attempt on your part to change how he deals with his problems and it will make him feel you don't trust him. Show a little concern and ignore the fact that he is upset. He will automatically come and talk, just give him space to get himself ready.

Also, avoid offering free advice because it will make him feel as if you don't accept who he is. Instead, be patient and have faith that he will be able to grow on his own and eventually he will come to you to ask for advice.

Another big mistake women make is to make sacrifices for their man, then expecting the same from them. However, this simply makes him feel as if you are trying to change the way he behaves. Therefore, you are better off doing things for yourself and not depending on him to make you happy.

Just as you wouldn't like your man making decisions for you or telling you what to do, your man will also feel as if you are trying to control him if you order him about. Relax and accept the imperfections that make life beautiful. After all, what's more important? His feelings or whether or not he vacuumed under the table?

## 8

## Men will be Men

While this might be considered a little shallow, unfortunately, there is nothing we can do about the fact that men are visual creatures. This doesn't mean that you have to stop by the plastic surgeon in the morning to remodel yourself into a Victoria's Secret runway model. Far from it.

However, there are certain things that make women much more attractive to men. For example, men absolutely adore long hair on women. It is a sign of femininity and the only thing they love more than long hair, is to see that long hair pulled up in a pony tail. The reason for this is because it has a slight sexual connotation by showing off the graceful curves of your neck.

Also, if you adopt a more feminine style by

wearing dresses and skirts more often, you will find that more men are attracted to you. This is simply because women tend to appear softer and more feminine in dresses and men are attracted to that like bees to honey.

Last but definitely not least, high heels. Yes, heels do something amazing for your posture and make men fall head over their proverbial heels. One reason is because you tend to move slower and more gracefully when you are wearing high heels. It's virtually impossible to walk at breakneck speed or be less than graceful in high heels. Not if you don't want to break your neck that is.

Also, you know you feel absolutely amazing inside when you are wearing heels. It gives you a new confidence because you feel taller and more attractive. You basically feel on top of the world. And this confidence shines through and men pick up on it. There's nothing more attractive to a man than a woman who is comfortable with herself and is confident.

## ೞ 9 ೞ

## Conquering the Bed

Sex is a vital part of any relationship and it can make or break an otherwise wonderful couple. The biggest problem women have when it comes to sex is that they tend to be overly self-conscious. This then leads on a lack of focus on what is going on and you tend to be so worried about how you look that you forget to enjoy what's happening.

Not only that, but some women also voice their insecurities which makes it even worse. Ladies, you need to stop focusing on what you think is wrong with you and enjoy the moment. If he's there with you and he is telling you that you turn him on then believe him. After all, guys can't fake it. Seriously, they can't.

If he's in the bedroom with you, then he's already turned on by who you are right now. Pointing out your cellulite or trying to hide a part of your body for fear you might look fat or wobbly is like shining a spotlight on it for him to see, where he probably would never have noticed otherwise. Men just don't see those things we think of as imperfections until you point them out.

Another problem many relationships run into is that sex becomes routine and then slowly dries up and disappears completely. Society is as much to blame for this as we are. We forget that sex is supposed to be fun as well as a great way to bond with your partner.

In one of Tony Robbins' seminars, he told the story of a couple who were in their nineties and had been together for more than sixty years. However, they were still deeply in love with each other and it showed because they expressed themselves physically as well. So much so that Tony suggested they might want to retire to their room. When asked what their secret was, the couple responded that, amongst other things, they would try anything once. If they liked it then they would do it again.

In other words, variety is the spice of life and sex is nothing to be ashamed of. The more variety you have in your sex life, the less likely it is that it will become boring and a matter of obligation rather than enjoyment.

There are so many things you can do to keep your sex life interesting, from surprising your man with an impromptu romp to role playing for him, you can be sure he will definitely want to play along. Remember that it doesn't always have to be a Hollywood production of the perfect romantic evening. Sometimes a hot, sweaty, fast roll in the hay is exactly what the doctor ordered. You'll also find that it is a great way to relieve tension as well.

However, don't expect to share a wonderful talk afterwards and then get upset when he falls asleep. Men are hard pressed to share their feelings at any time, let alone after a good round of sex when their brain has completely switched off.

## ෨ 10 ଔ

## Final Words

If you want to be the queen bee, the woman that all men adore, then you need to understand them. The more you understand about a man and how he processes and functions, the higher your chances of being able to personify his dream woman.

This doesn't mean that you should create a persona that is not in line with who you are. Unfortunately, though, many women are afraid to show their true selves because they feel it makes them look weak. The problem is that the more you hide your true self, the more resentment you build up inside, whether or not you realize it, because you are working so hard to put up this front that has nothing to do with who you really are.

If you love and accept who you are, you will give

off an aura of confidence that men find irresistible. And by allowing yourself to admit to the fact that you need a man in your life, you will suddenly feel liberated and will be more open. You won't project the hardened façade of "I don't need anyone" which drives most men away, because as we have already seen, men want to feel needed.

A man wants to take care of a woman. He wants to be her hero. A woman who is self-sufficient projects an aura of ruthless independence that will drive men away. Of course, there are men who like strong women who take the lead but more often than not, a woman, no matter how strong or independent she is, doesn't want to have to be the one doing the protecting. Even if she won't admit it to herself, initially.

The problem is that by being dishonest with yourself you might enter into a relationship that will end up hurting both of you. The reason is that in the beginning you project one thing. Then later on you open up and show your vulnerability and need for support. He will then feel cheated that you are a different person and so resentment will build up on both sides and lead to a sad ending.

So accept who you really are and allow yourself to be a woman. In fact, be proud of the fact that you are a woman and remember that men live to make their women happy because it's what makes them feel good.

The woman all men adore is one who isn't afraid to show her softer side, to show that she needs her man and one who understands the fundamental differences between men and women. By understanding how a man reacts differently she will be able to better respond to him and thus create a peaceful loving home.

There is nothing more attractive to a man than a woman who has enough confidence and trust in him to be vulnerable with him. He will move mountains to please you and put a smile on your face, because men melt when they see the woman they love smile.

# About The Author

Manhardeep Singh is an India-based best-selling author, motivational speaker, and handwriting analyst. Gaining from the experience of one-on-one counseling sessions, Manhardeep pens down self-help books. His writings are focused on the topics of handwriting analysis and bring the best out of life.

Manhardeep Singh has a Masters degree in Business Administration. He regularly writes articles in his blog www.manhardeep.com.

# Get Your Handwriting Analysis

I still remember that fine day when I used handwriting analysis to unveil that what was wrong in me was my "low self-esteem". I said NO to offers and barely had any friends. Working on my self-esteem using handwriting analysis changed my life completely. I gained confidence, attracted people like magnet and improved my life.

I invite you to grab this opportunity to know about what is stopping you or someone you know down from achieving the next level. Use the link below to get your handwriting analyzed:
https://www.fiverr.com/share/mYQV2N

# IN THE SAME SERIES

**DATING ESSENTIALS SERIES**

**ARE YOU RELATIONSHIP READY?**

KNOW IF YOU ARE READY FOR A SERIOUS RELATIONSHIP

MANHARDEEP SINGH

# MORE BOOKS FROM THE AUTHOR

## STANDALONES:

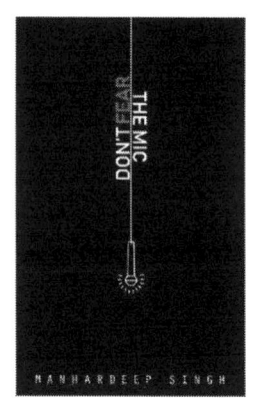

## HANDWRITING EXPERT SERIES:

## 99 FOR SELF SERIES:

# WIMPY KID SERIES:

# ONE-LINERS SERIES:

Made in the USA
Las Vegas, NV
05 June 2025